THE INTERNATIONAL
GARLIC
COOKBOOK

THE INTERNATIONAL
GARLIC
COOKBOOK

Food Photography by Steven Mark Needham

CollinsPublishersSanFrancisco

A Division of HarperCollins*Publishers*

First published in USA 1995 by Collins Publishers San Francisco
1160 Battery Street, San Francisco, CA 94111

Produced by Smallwood & Stewart, Inc.
New York City

© 1995 Smallwood & Stewart, Inc.

Editor: Mary MacVean

The international garlic cookbook / Food photography by
Steven Mark Needham.
p.   cm.
"Produced by Smallwood and Stewart, Inc."
Includes index.
ISBN 0-00-225056-X
1. Cookery (Garlic).   2. Cookery, International.
I. Smallwood and Stewart.   II. Collins Publishers San Francisco.
TX819.G3I58   1995   95-16656
641.6'526—dc20   CIP

Printed in China

1 3 5 7 9 10 8 6 4 2

Contents

Appetizers 10

Soups & Salads 25

Pastas & Noodles 32

Seafood 36

Poultry 50

Meat 62

Side Dishes 80

Conversion Tables 94

Index 95

Recipe & Photography Credits 96

Introduction

Egyptian slaves ate great quantities of it for strength and endurance as they built the Pyramids. Medieval peasants used it to ward off evil spirits. Folk healers have prescribed it for everything from colds to unrequited love. Soldiers in the First World War put its juice on bandages to fight infections. Scientists say it may help prevent heart disease and some cancers. And, by the way, it also happens to be one of the planet's most popular foods.

Garlic plays such a starring role in the world's cuisines, in the kitchens of professionals and home cooks alike, that it is almost impossible to imagine French or Italian, Mexican or Middle Eastern, Spanish or Chinese food without it. Surprisingly, it was disdained in the United States as unsavory peasant food as recently as the turn of the century, and was not grown here commercially until after the Second World War. But garlic's flavor ultimately won out over snobbery, and today Americans consume 164 million pounds of garlic a year ~ with meat, fish, and poultry, beans and pasta, vegetables and bread, even all by itself. Tens of thousands of people attend the annual Gilroy, California, Garlic Festival, savoring the bulb every way ~ even in ice cream.

Garlic can be eaten raw or cooked. Mincing and mashing release more of its oils and increase its pungency; cooking reduces it. It is a subtle background note in Mexican mole sauce, and a predominant flavor in fiery Thai red curry paste. The gentle, slightly sweet allure of roasted garlic, dressed with herbs and spices, is a far cry from the sharp insistence of aïoli. Mashed with basil and oil, it becomes pesto; combined with hot cayenne and herbs, it turns into the Moroccan sauce called charmoula; mix it with mashed potatoes, and an American classic gets a new face. A clove left for a few hours in a container of potato chips or added to the oil before making popcorn transforms those snacks. Steeped in vinegar, it lends its flavor to salad dressings.

Garlic might be perfect but for one significant blight: It isn't called the stinking rose for nothing. Its odor possesses such strength and aggression that it will literally ooze out of your pores if you feast on it too enthusiastically. (However, the aroma on your breath can be neutralized by chewing on parsley or a coffee bean.)

Cooking with Garlic

- The garlic harvest in California, the source of 90 percent of the nation's supply, runs from June to September. Bulbs are then dried before being sold. Buy garlic bulbs that are firm and plump with clean, dry, unbroken skins. Keep them in a cool, dry place, such as a mesh bag or ceramic garlic jar, but do not refrigerate them. Whole bulbs will keep up to two months, cloves for a few days. Always try to use fresh garlic; neither garlic powder nor garlic salt has the same flavor.

- If sprouts develop, you can still use the garlic, but first cut the clove in half and remove the sprout, which can taste bitter. (Garlic can also taste bitter if allowed to burn, so take care when sautéing.)

- Two medium cloves are considered equal to a teaspoon of minced garlic. But in all recipes, feel free to adjust the amount of garlic to taste.

- When mincing garlic, sprinkle it with a little of the salt called for in the recipe; this will keep the garlic pieces from sticking to your knife.

For most recipes, chop garlic by hand; a processor will mash the cloves. Use chopped garlic as soon as possible.

- In the recipes that follow, all garlic is to be peeled unless otherwise stated. To peel a clove of garlic, smash it lightly against a cutting board with the broad side of a large knife. To peel a large quantity of garlic, drop the cloves into boiling water for 30 seconds. Drain, rinse under cold water until cool, and slip off the skins.

- Peeled fresh garlic can be stored in olive oil, with some precautions. Keep the oil in the coldest part of the refrigerator, and use it and the garlic within a few days.

- To remove the smell of garlic from your skin, rub your fingers on a stainless steel spoon or bowl under running water, then wash with soap and water ~ the metal neutralizes the garlic.

- A note of caution about the use of raw eggs in some recipes: Salmonella can cause a serious illness that can be contracted from infected, uncooked eggs. Seek out a reliable source for your eggs, and consider buying them directly from a farmers' market.

Roasted Garlic

Whole garlic bulbs can be roasted in clay roasters, aluminum foil packets, or covered oven-proof dishes. The advantage of clay is that it allows the garlic to caramelize and take on sweeter notes. In foil or a covered dish, steam does some of the cooking. But in any container, ground spices or herb sprigs warmed in oil and poured over the bulb add depth of flavor. This recipe and the variations that follow are just a start; try other flavors to accent the garlic. Soft, spreadable roasted garlic is marvelous simply smeared on good bread, but try the other uses suggested below.

4 garlic bulbs with large,
    firm cloves
2 tablespoons olive oil
½ teaspoon hot chile oil

½ teaspoon chile powder
½ teaspoon ground cumin
Salt & black pepper

Remove most of the outer papery skin of the garlic bulb, leaving the bulb intact. Trim about a half inch off the top of each bulb to expose the cloves.

Gently heat the oils in a small saucepan. Add the spices and stir to moisten them. Remove the pan from the heat but keep the oil warm.

Cluster the garlic in the center of a clay roaster. Drizzle the bulbs with the warm oil, making sure to scrape the spices from the pan to coat the exposed cloves.

Add the salt and pepper to taste.

Cover the roaster with the domed lid. Place it in a cold oven and set the oven temperature to 350°F. Bake for 1 hour, basting the bulb with the juices. Cool slightly.

Separate the cloves from the bulb. Discard the skins. Spread the pulp on cornbread or on other bread or on vegetables, stir it into rice or sauces, or mix it with pureed beans for a dip.

Asian Roasted Garlic

Gently heat 2 tablespoons peanut oil, ¼ teaspoon dark sesame oil, 2 teaspoons soy sauce, and 1 tablespoon freshly grated, peeled ginger. Prepare the garlic as above and drizzle with the warm oil. Cook garlic as above, using 4 bulbs. Spread the pulp on mashed or baked sweet potatoes, other vegetables, or on chicken, beef, or pork just before they finish roasting.

New England Roasted Garlic

Maple syrup makes an unlikely but satisfying companion to roasted garlic, bringing out garlic's sweet nature.

Use 4 bulbs, 2 tablespoons maple syrup, and 2 teaspoons butter. Place the dry bulbs in the roaster, drizzle with the syrup, and dot with small pieces of the butter. Roast as above. Spread the pulp on muffins, under the skin of chicken before roasting, or add it to barbecue sauce for ribs.

Roasted Elephant Garlic

With just four or five cloves per bulb, elephant garlic has a lighter flavor and a stronger hint of onion than its smaller cousins. When the cloves are trimmed, the skins may become loose, but keep them in place for roasting.

Use 2 bulbs, 12 sprigs fresh rosemary or thyme, 2 tablespoons olive oil, and salt and freshly ground black pepper to taste. Gently heat the oil in a small saucepan. Add the herb sprigs and stir to coat them with oil. Remove the pan from the heat but keep the oil warm. Carefully separate the cloves at the root end and trim about ¼ inch from the top of each clove. Lay 6 herb sprigs in the clay roaster. Cluster the garlic cloves in a single layer over the herbs.

Drizzle with the warm oil and cover with the remaining herb sprigs. Generously season with salt and pepper. Roast as above, for 1¼ hours. Cool and discard the skins and herbs. Spread on bread, chicken, or fish.

BRUSCHETTA CON POMODORI

This appetizer is wildly popular all over Italy, and a similar snack is made without the basil in the Catalonia region of Spain. The Romans prefer to omit the topping entirely; they simply grill the rounds, preferably over hot coals, and brush them with the garlic-flavored oil. Bruschetta also makes an excellent accompaniment to a salad.

6 slices crusty Italian bread,
   halved crosswise

1 large garlic clove, minced

¼ cup extra-virgin
   olive oil

6 large firm ripe tomatoes,
   peeled, seeded & chopped

Salt & black pepper

¼ cup minced fresh basil

1 tablespoon balsamic vinegar

Preheat the broiler. Arrange the slices of bread on a baking sheet and broil 5 inches from the heat source until lightly browned. Turn and brown the other side.

In a small bowl, combine the garlic and 3 tablespoons of the oil, and brush the mixture on one side of the bread slices.

In a skillet, heat the remaining 1 tablespoon of oil over medium heat, add the tomatoes, and salt and pepper to taste; toss for 1 to 2 minutes, until the tomatoes are just heated through. Stir in the basil and vinegar. Top the toasted bread slices with the tomato mixture. **Serves 6.**

MARINATED GARLIC~HERBED OLIVES

*More olive trees grow in Andalusia in southern Spain
than anywhere else in the world, so olives are a favorite* tapa, *or
appetizer. The longer these olives marinate, the better
they become. They go particularly well with a glass of chilled
dry sherry, which also comes from Andalusia.*

One 1-pound jar large Spanish
   green olives with pits,
   drained & well rinsed

2 lemon wedges

2 tablespoons fruity
   extra-virgin olive oil

½ cup red wine vinegar

6 garlic cloves, lightly crushed

2 or 3 sprigs fresh thyme, or
   1 teaspoon dried

2 bay leaves

1 teaspoon dried oregano

½ teaspoon paprika

⅛ teaspoon black pepper

1 teaspoon cumin seeds,
   crushed, or ground cumin

1 teaspoon fennel seeds

With a sharp knife, make a small slit in each olive to allow the marinade to penetrate. Place the olives in a glass jar. Add the remaining ingredients and enough water to completely cover the olives. Cover the jar. Shake well, refrigerate, and allow to marinate for at least a few days, preferably for more than 2 weeks. The olives will keep in the refrigerator for many months. **Makes about 3 cups.**

STEAMED ARTICHOKES WITH GARLIC~BASIL AÏOLI

Steaming is a particularly good way to prepare artichokes because it seals in both flavor and nutrients. Served with a garlicky basil mayonnaise, steamed artichokes are delicious warm or chilled. They are perfect for informal summer entertaining.

6 medium to large artichokes, about 10 ounces each
1 lemon, sliced
1 tablespoon olive oil
1 teaspoon salt

Garlic-Basil Aïoli:

1 cup fresh basil
6 garlic cloves
1 large egg
1½ teaspoons fresh lemon juice
1 cup mild extra-virgin olive oil
Fresh chives, for garnish (optional)

Using a sharp knife, cut off the stems of the artichokes flush with the bottoms and pull off the leaves at the base. Trim off the remaining sharp leaf tips with kitchen scissors. Rub the freshly cut parts with a lemon slice to prevent discoloration.

Set a steamer rack in a large saucepan or Dutch oven and fill with water to just below the rack. Add the remaining lemon slices, oil, and salt. Set the artichokes upright on the rack in the pan.

Cover and steam over medium heat for 35 to 45 minutes, until the leaves pull off easily.

Meanwhile, prepare the aïoli: In a food processor fitted with the metal blade, combine the basil, garlic, egg, and lemon juice, and process until pureed. With the motor running, gradually add the oil through the feed tube in a thin steady stream until combined. Transfer to a small bowl and set aside.

Drain the artichokes upside down in

a colander. When cool enough through-out to handle, carefully spread the outer leaves of each artichoke to expose the choke. Remove and discard the small leaves in the center and scrape out the fuzzy choke with a spoon.

To serve, place the artichokes on individual serving plates. Fill the arti-choke centers with some of the aïoli, for dipping the leaves. Garnish the aïoli with the chives, if desired. Pass any remaining aïoli at the table. **Serves 6.**

17

TAPENADE

*Anchovies, olives, capers, fresh herbs, and garlic ~ these are the beloved,
bold ingredients of the cuisine of southern France, and Provence
in particular. They are all used in* tapenade, *a thick paste that makes
a wonderful spread, dip, or even a filling for hard-boiled eggs.*

One 2-ounce can flat anchovy
    fillets, drained & patted dry

1 cup black olives, preferably
    oil-cured or Calamata, pitted

2 tablespoons drained capers

1 teaspoon minced fresh thyme,
    or ¼ teaspoon dried

1 teaspoon minced fresh
    rosemary, or ¼ teaspoon
    dried

2 large garlic cloves, chopped

2 to 3 teaspoons fresh
    lemon juice

¼ cup extra-virgin olive oil

Black pepper

In a food processor fitted with the metal blade, combine the anchovies, olives, capers, thyme, rosemary, garlic, and lemon juice to taste, and process until smooth. With the motor running, add the oil in a stream. Transfer the spread to a small bowl and season with the pepper to taste. Serve at room temperature with toasted bread rounds or crudités. **Makes about 1 cup.**

BABA GHANNOUJ

Roasted eggplant and tahini (sesame paste) give this Middle Eastern dish
its distinct smoky flavor. In Lebanon it is often garnished with pomegranate seeds, but
the more readily available garnish of parsley and olive oil called for here
is excellent. Serve this spread with fresh pita or other Middle Eastern flatbreads.
It will keep several days in the refrigerator in an airtight container.

1 large eggplant
2 tablespoons olive oil, plus
   1 teaspoon for garnish
2 garlic cloves, minced
3 tablespoons lemon juice

2¼ tablespoons tahini
   (sesame paste)
½ teaspoon salt
¼ cup chopped fresh flat-leaf
   parsley, plus 1 tablespoon
   for garnish

Preheat the oven to 450°F. With a fork or paring knife, prick the eggplant in several places, then place it on a baking sheet. Bake for 35 minutes, until the eggplant has collapsed and the pulp is soft. When the eggplant is cool enough to handle, scrape the pulp into a food processor fitted with the metal blade. Discard the skin.

In a small skillet, heat 2 tablespoons of the oil over low heat. Add the garlic and cook for 2 minutes, until soft.

Add the garlic and oil, lemon juice, tahini, and salt to the eggplant. Process for 1 minute, until smooth. Add the ¼ cup parsley and process for 20 seconds longer. Serve at room temperature, garnished with the remaining parsley and drizzled with the remaining oil. **Makes 2 cups.**

GARLIC SHRIMP

This richly flavored favorite Spanish tapa *is served
sizzling hot in shallow earthenware casseroles called* cazuelas.
Good crusty bread is a must for dunking in the sauce.

¾ pound small shrimp
   in their shells
Salt
4 tablespoons olive oil
4 garlic cloves, sliced

1 small dried red chile pepper,
   cut in half & seeded, or ¼
   teaspoon hot-pepper flakes
1 tablespoon lemon juice
1 tablespoon dry white wine
2 tablespoons minced fresh
   flat-leaf parsley

Shell the shrimp. (It is not necessary to devein them.) Sprinkle with the salt to taste.

Heat the oil, garlic, and chile pepper in a shallow flameproof casserole over medium-high heat. When the garlic is just beginning to brown, add the shrimp and cook, stirring, for about 1 minute, until the shrimp are just done and firm to the touch. Stir in the lemon juice, wine, and parsley. Serve immediately, preferably in the casserole. **Serves 4 to 6.**

CLAMS WITH GARLIC AND WHITE WINE

The clams used for this dish, which is found in most tapas *bars in Spain, should be as small as possible. Use littleneck clams or cockles, and serve good fresh bread to mop up the garlicky green sauce.*

2 dozen small clams,
   thoroughly scrubbed
1 tablespoon cornmeal or flour
3 tablespoons olive oil
¼ cup minced onion
4 garlic cloves, minced

½ cup dry white wine
¼ cup fish broth
1 tablespoon lemon juice
1 bay leaf
3 tablespoons minced
   fresh parsley
Black pepper

To rid the clams of sand, place in a large bowl, cover with salted cold water, and sprinkle with cornmeal or flour. Refrigerate uncovered for several hours.

Drain, rinse, and dry the clams. Heat the oil in a large, shallow flameproof casserole, add the onion and garlic, and sauté over high heat. Just before the garlic begins to brown, add the clams and cook, stirring, for about 3 minutes. Add the wine and let it cook off. Stir in the fish broth, lemon juice, bay leaf, 1 tablespoon of the parsley, and pepper to taste. Reduce the heat to medium, cover, and cook, removing the clams as they open to a warm platter; add a little water if the liquid evaporates before all the clams have opened. (The finished dish should have some sauce.) Return the opened clams to the casserole, heat for 1 minute, and sprinkle with the remaining parsley. **Serves 6 to 8.**

Salsa Verde

Picante, or spicy, describes this flavorful Mexican sauce of fresh ingredients ~ tomatillos, jalapeño chiles, onions, and garlic ~ that are roasted for richness, pureed, then combined with a bold measure of pungent cilantro. When buying tomatillos, look for those that are bright green and hard to the touch, not yellow or soft. While this salsa was created to be served with tortilla chips, it is also very good as a garnish on chicken, fish, or meat.

1½ pounds tomatillos, husked & rinsed
1¼ cups chopped onions
4 large garlic cloves
3 or 4 jalapeño chiles, stemmed
3 tablespoons vegetable oil

1 teaspoon coarse salt
½ teaspoon black pepper
½ cup coarsely chopped fresh cilantro

Preheat the oven to 450°F. In a large bowl toss together the tomatillos, onions, garlic, chiles, oil, salt, and pepper. Transfer the mixture to a small baking pan and roast for 45 minutes. Remove from the oven and let cool.

In a food processor fitted with the metal blade, pulse the tomatillo mixture until coarse. Add the cilantro and pulse 3 or 4 times to combine. Serve immediately, or cover and refrigerate for up to 3 days. **Makes 3½ cups.**

GARLIC SOUP

*This Spanish peasant soup, in its simplest rendition, relies
upon the most basic of ingredients: water, garlic, and bread. The
broth, ham, and paprika give it greater depth of flavor.*

7 cups chicken broth

2 beef bones

1 garlic bulb, separated into
cloves, unpeeled, plus 8
cloves, peeled & chopped

4 fresh flat-leaf parsley sprigs

Salt & black pepper

2½ to 3 tablespoons olive oil

¼ pound cured ham, such as
prosciutto, sliced ¼ inch
thick & diced

1 tablespoon paprika

½ teaspoon ground cumin

8 bread slices from a long
narrow loaf, ¼ inch thick

4 large eggs (optional)

In a large saucepan, combine the broth, bones, the unpeeled garlic, parsley, and salt and pepper to taste. Bring to a boil, reduce the heat to medium and simmer, uncovered, for 30 minutes. Strain the soup into another saucepan. (You should have about 6 cups.)

Meanwhile, heat 1 tablespoon of the oil in a medium-size skillet and sauté the chopped garlic over medium heat until lightly golden. Add the ham and cook for 1 minute. Stir in the paprika and cumin, then immediately remove from the heat. Add the garlic mixture to the soup and simmer.

Preheat the oven to 350°F. Arrange the bread slices on a baking sheet and brush both sides lightly with the remaining oil. Bake, turning once, until golden on both sides, about 5 minutes.

Place the toasted bread in a soup tureen and pour in the hot soup. (If adding eggs, use a heatproof tureen, slide them into the soup, and bake at 450°F until set, about 3 to 4 minutes.) **Serves 4.**

FRENCH VEGETABLE SOUP WITH GARLIC PISTOU

This is the Provençal version of minestrone. Full of vegetables, it is hearty enough to be enjoyed as a main dish. The basil-garlic pistou *(the French version of Italy's pesto) that is swirled in should not be heated, but added just before the soup is served. Both tradition and taste dictate that it be made in a mortar with a pestle, not a food processor.*

2 tablespoons olive oil

1 cup chopped onions

2 leeks (white & tender green parts), rinsed & thinly sliced

3 garlic cloves, thinly sliced

1½ cups chopped tomatoes

1 cup cooked white kidney beans (cannellini)

1 medium carrot, halved lengthwise & thinly sliced

2 teaspoons salt

1 cup green beans cut into 1-inch lengths

1 medium zucchini, halved lengthwise & thinly sliced

1 cup (3 ounces) uncooked elbow macaroni

Pistou:

4 garlic cloves

¼ teaspoon salt

¼ cup fresh basil

⅓ cup grated Parmesan cheese

3 tablespoons olive oil

In a Dutch oven, heat the oil over low heat. Add the onions and cook, stirring occasionally, for 7 minutes, until soft. Add the leeks and garlic and cook for 2 minutes. Add the tomatoes, white beans, carrot, salt, and 10 cups of water. Heat to boiling over medium-high heat, then reduce the heat and simmer for 30 minutes. Add the green beans, zucchini, and macaroni, and simmer for 15 minutes.

Meanwhile, make the pistou: In a mortar with a pestle, pound the garlic and salt until mashed. Add the basil and pound until well combined. Transfer to a small bowl. Add the cheese and oil and beat with a fork until creamy.

To serve, spoon into serving bowls and stir in the pistou. **Serves 8.**

Mexican Garlic~Black Bean Soup

In Mexico, beans sustain; they are inexpensive and highly nutritional. This rich and spicy black bean soup calls for chiles de árbol ~ *fiery hot dried peppers* ~ *chicken stock, and herbs and spices for flavor and sophistication. If you can find it, by all means add the* epazote, *a pungent wild herb available in Latino markets. You may also discover* canela, *the Spanish name for the soft, multi-layered stick of Ceylon cinnamon.*

1 sprig fresh thyme, or
 ¼ teaspoon dried

1 sprig fresh oregano, or
 ¼ teaspoon dried

¼ ounce fresh epazote
 (optional)

¼ cup lard or vegetable oil

3 or 4 chiles de árbol, or 2
 teaspoons hot-pepper flakes

1½ cups chopped onions

8 garlic cloves, minced

1 pound smoked pork shanks

½ teaspoon freshly ground
 toasted cumin seeds

½ teaspoon ground coriander

¼ teaspoon ground canela, or
 ⅛ teaspoon cinnamon

Pinch of ground cloves

1 pound dried black beans,
 picked over & rinsed

8 cups chicken broth

2 or 3 tablespoons red wine
 vinegar or sherry vinegar

1 to 2 teaspoons coarse salt

Slivered red onions, for garnish

Tie the fresh herbs and epazote, if desired, into a bundle with string; set aside. Melt the lard or heat the oil in a 4-quart saucepan over medium-high heat and sauté the chiles for 30 seconds, until darkened but not burned. Add the onions and garlic and sauté for about 3 minutes, until softened. Add the pork

shanks and the herb bundle, or the dried herbs if using. Stir in the spices, beans, and chicken broth, and combine well. Bring to a boil over medium-high heat. Reduce the heat and simmer uncovered for 1¼ hours, stirring occasionally, until the beans are soft. Add the vinegar and salt and simmer for 30 minutes longer. Remove the pork shanks and herb bundle. Remove the chiles if desired. Serve in soup bowls and garnish with red onions. **Serves 4 to 6.**

Gazpacho a la Andaluza

There are few things more refreshing on a hot summer's day
than a chilled bowl of gazpacho. Often called liquid salad, this piquant
soup is very low in calories but filled with nutrients. It's
essential to use the best tomatoes you can find, whether fresh or canned.

1 pound fresh tomatoes,
  cut into pieces

1 pound canned plum tomatoes,
  with their juice

1 green bell pepper, cored,
  seeded & cut into pieces

2 teaspoons sugar

¼ teaspoon ground cumin

¼ cup sherry vinegar, or 5 tablespoons red wine vinegar

2 tablespoons olive oil

1 cup cold water

2 kirby cucumbers, or
  1 small cucumber,
  peeled & cut into pieces

½ small onion, halved

2 garlic cloves, chopped

Salt

Small croutons & finely
  chopped tomato, cucumber
  & green bell pepper,
  for garnish (optional)

In a food processor fitted with the metal blade, combine all the ingredients except the garnish in batches and process until pureed. Strain into a large bowl, pressing the solids with the back of a spoon to extract all the liquid.

Add more salt and vinegar to taste. Cover and refrigerate for several hours or overnight. (The gazpacho gains in flavor if chilled overnight.) If desired, garnish the soup just before serving. **Serves 6.**

CAESAR SALAD WITH GARLIC CROUTONS

Here is a garlic infused variation on the classic salad.

Garlic Croutons:

2 tablespoons olive oil

2 garlic cloves, crushed

5 slices French bread, crusts removed, cut into ½-inch cubes

Caesar Dressing:

4 garlic cloves, chopped

6 anchovy fillets, drained

1 teaspoon Worcestershire sauce

1 large egg yolk

1 tablespoon fresh lemon juice

¼ teaspoon salt

¼ teaspoon black pepper

⅓ cup extra-virgin olive oil

2 small heads romaine lettuce, separated into leaves

1 cup grated Parmesan cheese

Make the croutons: In a medium-size skillet, heat the oil over medium heat. Add the garlic and cook, stirring frequently, for 2 minutes, until golden. Remove and discard the garlic. Add the bread cubes, tossing to coat with the oil, and cook, stirring frequently, for 4 minutes, until golden. Remove to paper towels to drain.

Make the dressing: In a food processor fitted with the metal blade, combine all the dressing ingredients except the oil and process until well blended. With the motor running, gradually add the oil through the feed tube in a thin steady stream until combined.

In a large bowl, toss together the lettuce, cheese, and croutons. Add the dressing, tossing to coat. Transfer the salad to individual serving plates. **Serves 4.**

FETTUCCINE AL PESTO

*There are few sauces that compare with this renowned basil, garlic,
Parmesan, and pine nut creation from Genoa. Because the ingredients in the sauce
are not cooked, be sure to use the freshest basil and the best olive oil
and Parmesan available. Fettuccine is the perfect partner for this sauce, catching
and holding on to it. Pesto is also delicious over a salad or as a dip.*

Pesto:

2 cups fresh basil

4 garlic cloves, chopped

½ cup grated Parmesan,
   preferably Parmigiano-
   Reggiano

⅔ cup extra-virgin olive oil

¼ cup pine nuts

Salt & black pepper

Pasta:

1 pound fettuccine

Fresh basil, for garnish

Make the pesto: In a food processor fitted with the metal blade, combine all the ingredients and process until thoroughly combined.

Make the pasta: Bring a large pot of salted water to a boil. Add the fettuccine and cook, stirring occasionally, until al dente. Drain the pasta, transfer it to a heated serving bowl, and toss it with the pesto. Garnish with the fresh basil and serve at once. **Serves 4 to 6.**

SPAGHETTI WITH ROASTED EGGPLANT AND TOMATOES

In the extensive repertoire of Italian sauces, there are many that combine eggplant and tomatoes. This one is particularly appealing because the eggplant is roasted rather than fried, which is the more usual preparation. What you end up with is lighter but no less delicious.

1 to 1¼ pounds eggplant, trimmed & halved lengthwise

⅓ cup olive oil

1 onion, minced

4 large garlic cloves, minced

One 28-ounce can crushed tomatoes in puree

Salt & black pepper

2 tablespoons minced fresh basil

1 pound spaghetti

Preheat the oven to 400°F. Arrange the eggplant, cut side down, on an oiled baking sheet and bake until tender, about 20 to 25 minutes. Let cool, remove the skin, and coarsely chop the pulp.

In a skillet over medium heat, warm the oil until hot. Add the onion and garlic and cook, stirring, for 3 minutes. Add the tomatoes with puree and simmer, stirring occasionally, for 10 to 12 minutes, until thick. Add the chopped eggplant and salt and pepper to taste, and simmer, stirring occasionally, for 5 minutes, until heated through. Stir in the basil. Keep the sauce warm.

Bring a large pot of salted water to a boil. Add the spaghetti and cook, stirring occasionally, until al dente. Drain the pasta, transfer it to a heated serving bowl, and toss gently with the sauce. **Serves 4 to 6.**

COLD SESAME NOODLES WITH CHICKEN

This classic combination is especially popular in the Shanghai and Sichuan provinces of China. Chinese sesame paste, available in Asian food shops, is rich and deep brown in color.

1 pound Chinese egg noodles, ⅛-inch thick

2 tablespoons sesame oil

One 1-inch piece ginger

3 garlic cloves

¼ cup Chinese sesame paste

¼ cup chicken broth

3 tablespoons soy sauce

2 teaspoons sugar

1 teaspoon white rice vinegar

½ to 1 teaspoon chile paste

¼ pound cooked chicken, shredded

½ cup julienned cucumber

½ cup bean sprouts, rinsed & drained

¼ cup minced scallions (white & tender green parts)

Bring a large pot of water to a boil. Add the noodles and cook for 3 to 5 minutes, until al dente. Drain, rinse under cold water, and drain well again. In a large bowl, toss the noodles with 1 tablespoon of the oil. Cover and refrigerate.

In a food processor fitted with the metal blade, finely chop the ginger and garlic. Add the sesame paste and chicken broth and pulse, scraping down the sides of the bowl, for 3 to 4 seconds, until combined. Add the soy sauce, remaining oil, sugar, vinegar, and chile paste, and pulse to combine.

Add half the sesame sauce to the noodles and toss to combine. Divide the noodles among 4 bowls. Garnish each bowl with equal amounts of chicken, cucumber, and bean sprouts. Divide the remaining sauce among the bowls and sprinkle with the scallions. **Serves 4 to 6.**

THAI NOODLE SALAD

Fresh cilantro, basil, and mint are critical to the flavor of this dish.

Spicy Ginger-Garlic Dressing:

5 garlic cloves, minced

One 1-inch piece ginger, peeled & minced

¼ cup fresh lime juice

1 tablespoon *nam pla* (Thai fish sauce)

1 small jalapeño chile, seeded & finely chopped

1 tablespoon sugar

½ teaspoon salt

¾ cup canola oil

Thai Salad:

8 ounces dried vermicelli

4 scallions, cut into thin strips (white & tender green parts)

1 small carrot, cut into thin strips

2 tablespoons chopped fresh basil

2 tablespoons chopped fresh cilantro

2 tablespoons chopped fresh mint

4 to 6 lettuce leaves

Make the dressing: In a food processor fitted with the metal blade, combine all the ingredients except the oil and process until blended. With the motor running, gradually add the oil through the feed tube in a thin, steady stream until combined. Set aside.

Make the salad: Bring a large pot of salted water to a boil over high heat. Cook the vermicelli in the boiling water for 8 to 10 minutes, or until al dente; drain well.

In a medium-size bowl, combine the vermicelli, scallions, carrot, basil, cilantro, and mint. Add the dressing and toss to coat. To serve, arrange the lettuce leaves on serving plates, and spoon the salad on top. **Serves 4 to 6.**

MOROCCAN GRILLED FISH

The ingredients for charmoula, *a lusty Moroccan fish marinade, vary somewhat from household to household, but fresh cilantro is always a must.* Charmoula *is also used to season* tagines *(North African stews) and soups.*

Charmoula:

1 cup chopped fresh cilantro

⅓ cup chopped fresh parsley

3 garlic cloves, crushed

⅓ cup lemon juice

3 tablespoons olive oil

1 teaspoon ground cumin

½ teaspoon sweet paprika

¼ teaspoon salt

⅛ teaspoon cayenne

Four 6-ounce fillets of sea bass, red snapper, or grouper

Make the charmoula: In a food processor fitted with the metal blade, combine the cilantro, parsley, and garlic, and process until fine. Add the lemon juice, oil, cumin, paprika, salt, and cayenne, and process until smooth.

Place the fish fillets in a single layer in a large shallow pan or baking dish.

Spread the sauce over the fillets. Cover and refrigerate for several hours or overnight.

Preheat the broiler, with the pan 4 inches from the heat source. Broil the fish for 4 to 5 minutes, until it flakes when tested with a fork. **Serves 4.**

BOURRIDE

Garlic fans may find this Provençal fish stew superior to its better-known cousin, bouillabaisse. Creamy with the eggs and garlic of the aïoli, bourride has neither shellfish nor tomato, and is an elegant, simple dish to make for company.

Aïoli:

6 garlic cloves

¼ teaspoon salt

2 large egg yolks

1 cup extra-virgin olive oil

2 tablespoons lemon juice

Fish Broth & Stew:

2½ pounds fish bones, from any white-fleshed fish, cut into large pieces

1 large onion, thinly sliced

1 large leek (white & tender green parts), rinsed & thinly sliced

1 large carrot, thinly sliced

1 stalk celery, thinly sliced

2 sprigs fresh thyme

½ teaspoon fennel seeds

1 bay leaf

Two 3 x ½-inch strips orange zest

½ cup dry white wine

½ teaspoon salt

1 pound all-purpose potatoes, peeled & thinly sliced

2½ pounds assorted firm-fleshed white fish such as halibut, cod, snapper, or bass, skin left on, cut into large chunks

2 large egg yolks

8 slices thick French bread, toasted

2 tablespoons snipped fresh chives

Make the aïoli: In a small bowl, using the back of a spoon, mash the garlic and salt to a smooth paste. Stir in the egg yolks, then whisk in half of the oil, drop by drop, until it has been incorporated. Add the lemon juice and stir in the remaining oil until the mixture is glossy and the consistency of mayonnaise. Set aside.

Make the fish broth & stew: In a

stockpot, combine the fish bones, onion, leek, carrot, celery, thyme, fennel, bay leaf, orange zest, wine, salt, and 8 cups of cold water. Bring to a boil. Reduce the heat and simmer for 45 minutes, skimming off any scum that rises to the surface. Strain the broth.

Return the broth to the pot and bring to a boil over high heat. Add the potatoes and cook for 5 minutes. Reduce the heat to medium-low, add the fish, and simmer for 10 minutes, until the fish is just cooked through. Transfer the fish and potatoes to a platter and keep warm.

In a medium-size bowl, whisk together the aïoli and the egg yolks. Gradually whisk in ½ cup of the broth. Whisk the aïoli mixture back into the broth and simmer for 3 to 4 minutes, until it is thick and creamy; be sure that it does not boil. Place each slice of toasted bread in a warm soup bowl and spoon the fish and potatoes on top. Ladle the broth over and sprinkle with the chives. **Serves 8.**

NORTH BEACH CIOPPINO

*Cioppino, a seafood stew, has been attributed to Portuguese and Italian
fishermen who have fished the northern California coast for more
than a century. Dungeness crab is a Pacific variety and can be hard to find live
away from the West. Frozen whole cooked crab can be used if need be.*

1 cooked Dungeness crab
(about 1½ to 2 pounds)

2 tablespoons olive oil

1 large onion, chopped

3 garlic cloves, minced

1 large green bell pepper,
seeded & chopped

2½ cups canned tomatoes,
coarsely chopped & drained

2 tablespoons tomato paste

¼ teaspoon dried basil

¼ teaspoon dried oregano

¼ teaspoon dried thyme

¼ cup chopped fresh parsley

2 cups dry red wine, such as
cabernet sauvignon

1 teaspoon salt

½ teaspoon black pepper

1 pound rock cod or haddock,
cut into 2-inch pieces

1 dozen littleneck or
cherrystone clams

1 dozen large shrimp

Pull the legs from the crab and gently crack them. Working over a shallow bowl to collect the juices, remove the crab body from the shell and clean off the gills and fibrous gray matter attached to it; discard the shell. Scrape the yellow crab butter from the body and add it to the juices in the bowl. Cut the body into quarters and set aside.

In a Dutch oven, heat the oil over medium-high heat. Add the onion, garlic, and bell pepper and cook, stirring frequently, for 5 minutes, until the vegetables begin to soften. Add the tomatoes, breaking them up with a spoon, and cook, stirring frequently, for 5 minutes. Stir in the tomato paste, crab juices, herbs, wine, salt, and

pepper, and cook over medium heat, stirring occasionally, for 20 minutes.

Add the cod and clams and cook, stirring occasionally, for 5 minutes. Add the shrimp and cook, covered, for 5 minutes. Add the crab and cook, covered, for 5 minutes more, until the clams have opened and the shrimp have turned pink and opaque.

Ladle the soup into individual serving bowls and serve. **Serves 6 to 8.**

STEAMED MUSSELS LAYERED WITH THAI HERBS

Clay pot cooking, a technique perfected by the Chinese, is well suited to seafood. In this simple Thai dish, mussels, layered with fragrant herbs, are steamed open to remain briny, succulent, and sweet. Finally, sparked with a garlic-chile condiment ~ there are six garlic cloves and up to eight chiles in the paste! ~ they are truly set afire. Thai basil and kaffir lime leaves are available in Asian food markets.

2½ pounds mussels, debearded & scrubbed

1 cup fish broth

4 stalks lemongrass, cut into 2-inch pieces

8 medium shallots, thinly sliced

½ cup fresh Thai basil

9 fresh kaffir lime leaves, center vein of each removed

8 garlic cloves, chopped

3 to 4 small red chile peppers, chopped

3 to 4 small green chile peppers, chopped

1 teaspoon salt

½ teaspoon sugar

3 to 4 tablespoons lemon juice

2 tablespoons chopped fresh cilantro

Rinse the mussels in several changes of cold water. Discard any that have opened. Drain.

Pour the fish broth into a 2½-quart clay pot. In alternate layers in the pot, arrange roughly one third of the mussels, one third of the lemongrass, one third of the shallots, one third of the basil, and one third of the lime leaves. Continue to make layers with the remaining mussels, lemongrass, shallots, basil, and lime leaves. Cover the pot and bring to a boil over low heat, for 2 to 3 minutes. Increase the heat to high for 5 to 6

minutes, until the mussels have fully opened. Discard any that do not open.

In a mortar with a pestle, pound the garlic, chile peppers, salt, and sugar until they form a paste. Stir in the lemon juice and sprinkle with the cilantro. Spoon a dab of paste on each mussel or serve the paste alongside the mussels. **Serves 4.**

Scallops with Vegetables and Spicy Sauce

This stir-fry from the western part of China is hot, but not fiery. For the courageous, add more chile paste and chile peppers.

2 tablespoons soy sauce

2 teaspoons plus 1 tablespoon rice wine

2 tablespoons plus 2 teaspoons cornstarch

2½ teaspoons sugar

1½ pounds sea scallops, rinsed & drained

¼ cup chicken broth

2 teaspoons oyster sauce

1 teaspoon sesame oil

½ teaspoon chile paste

½ pound snow peas, strings removed

¼ cup peanut oil

4 whole dried red chile peppers

4 pieces dried orange peel

1 star anise

4 slices ginger, peeled

5 garlic cloves, crushed

4 scallions, cut into 2-inch sections

2 large red bell peppers, seeded & cut into 1-inch cubes

Cut up any large scallops so that all scallops are approximately the same size. In a large bowl, combine well 1 tablespoon of the soy sauce, 2 teaspoons of the rice wine, 2 tablespoons of the cornstarch, and ½ teaspoon of the sugar. Mix in the scallops. Cover loosely with plastic wrap. In another bowl, combine the chicken broth, the remaining soy sauce, the remaining rice wine, remaining cornstarch, remaining sugar, and the oyster sauce, sesame oil, and chile paste.

In a saucepan of lightly salted water, blanch the snow peas for 1 to 2 minutes, until they turn bright green. Refresh under cold water and drain.

Heat 3 tablespoons of the peanut oil in a wok over high heat until it just begins to smoke. Reduce the heat to medium-high, carefully add the chile peppers, orange peel, and star anise, and cook for 1 to 2 minutes, until the ingredients have charred. With a slotted spoon, carefully remove them and discard.

Increase the heat to high and add half the scallops. Stir-fry rapidly for 3 to 4 minutes, until the scallops are firm and slightly browned. Remove with a slotted spoon to a plate. Repeat with the remaining scallops. Without cleaning the wok, add the remaining peanut oil, the ginger, garlic, scallions, and bell peppers. Stir-fry rapidly for 2 to 3 minutes, until the peppers begin to soften. Restir the broth mixture and swirl it into the wok. Add the scallops and snow peas and stir-fry rapidly for 1 to 2 minutes, until the scallops are heated through and the sauce has thickened slightly. **Serves 4 to 6.**

GRILLED ACHIOTE SHRIMP

*To make this Mexican dish, you will need skewers, as well as
condimento de achiote, a paste made from seeds of the annatto tree,
ground chiles, and cumin, available in Latin food markets. The
condimento colors the shrimp a remarkable red-orange and flavors
them with the distinctive musky aroma of the annatto seed.*

3 tablespoons vegetable oil

3 large garlic cloves

Three 4-ounce packages
condimento de achiote,
crumbled

3 tablespoons frozen orange
juice concentrate, thawed

½ cup fresh grapefruit juice

1 tablespoon cider vinegar

1 teaspoon freshly ground
toasted cumin seeds

1 teaspoon freshly ground
coriander seeds

1 teaspoon freshly ground
canela, or ½ teaspoon
cinnamon

¼ teaspoon freshly
ground cloves

½ teaspoon black pepper

About 3 pounds extra-large
shrimp, shelled & deveined

Arroz Mexicana (p. 86), hot

Heat the oil in a skillet over medium-high heat; sauté the garlic for 3 to 4 minutes, until golden brown. Let cool, then transfer the garlic and oil to a food processor fitted with the metal blade. Add the condimento de achiote, orange juice and grapefruit juice, vinegar, 3 tablespoons of cold water, cumin, coriander, canela, cloves, and pepper, and process until smooth. Pour the mixture into a large bowl, add the shrimp, and stir to coat well. Cover and let the shrimp marinate in the refrigerator overnight.

Preheat a grill or broiler, with the rack 4 inches from the heat source. Soak twelve 8-inch bamboo skewers in water

for 20 minutes. Thread 3 shrimp through the middle on each skewer; they should form three "C" shapes in a row on each skewer. Grill or broil the shrimp for about 2 minutes on each side, until cooked through. Divide the hot rice among 6 serving plates, top with 1 or 2 skewers of shrimp, and serve. **Serves 6.**

HOT AND SOUR SHRIMP WITH CUCUMBER CURRY

Thai curries are remarkably individualistic; they differ not only in color,
but also in texture. This is one of the lighter ones: The broth is sour
but also has spirited sweet, salty, and hot overtones with a strong garlic and
tamarind flavor. You'll need a wok to prepare this dish.

6 dried red chile peppers

1 cucumber

½ cup tamarind pulp soaked in
   1 cup warm water

6 garlic cloves, chopped

3 medium shallots, chopped

1 teaspoon salt

1 pound medium shrimp,
   shelled & deveined

2 teaspoons shrimp paste

2 teaspoons sugar

1 tablespoon *nam pla*
   (Thai fish sauce)

Soak the chile peppers in warm water to cover for 1 hour, until just softened. Drain and discard the water. Cut designs into the peel of the cucumber, then halve the cucumber lengthwise and cut into bite-size pieces. Strain the tamarind pulp, setting aside the pulp and juice.

In a food processor fitted with the metal blade, combine the chile peppers, garlic, shallots, and salt until smooth. Gradually add 1 to 2 tablespoons of cold water to assist the blending.

In a wok over medium-high heat, bring 1 cup of water and the chile-garlic paste to a boil. Add 5 shrimp and cook for 1 to 2 minutes, until orange and just firm. Remove with a slotted spoon to the food processor and pulse until finely chopped. Set aside.

Add the shrimp paste and 1 cup of cold water to the wok and bring to a boil. Add the cucumber and half the tamarind

juice and bring to a boil. Add the remaining tamarind juice and fresh shrimp, the ground shrimp, sugar, and nam pla. Add 1 cup of cold water to the reserved tamarind pulp. Re-strain and add the juice to the wok. Bring to a boil and cook for 2 to 3 minutes, until the shrimp is orange and just firm. Remove immediately from the heat and serve. **Serves 4.**

THAI GRILLED GARLIC CHICKEN

Thai cooks have expertly refined the art of grilling. Here, chicken legs are put in a marinade inspired by Indian cuisine, boldly flavored and colored with turmeric. When grilled, the chicken turns a beautiful shade of ocher. Serve it with bottled **naam** jim kai, *a pickled chile sauce with garlic and plums available in Asian food markets.*

4 whole chicken legs with skin, each broken at the joint, rinsed & patted dry
16 coriander roots
½ teaspoon black pepper
1 teaspoon salt

16 garlic cloves, chopped
1 teaspoon ground turmeric
1 teaspoon sugar
1 to 3 tablespoons vegetable oil
2 tablespoons coconut milk
Naam jim kai, for garnish

Cut ½-inch-deep slits randomly all over the chicken legs to allow the marinade to easily penetrate the meat. Place on a broiler pan and set aside.

In a food processor fitted with the metal blade, pulse the coriander roots, pepper, salt, garlic, turmeric, and sugar until just smooth. If necessary, add the oil to assist in blending. Stir in the coconut milk until well combined.

Spread the marinade over the chicken and under the skin, cover, and refrigerate for at least 2 to 3 hours, or preferably overnight.

Preheat the grill or broiler. Arrange the chicken 4 inches from the heat source and grill or broil for 10 to 12 minutes on each side, until cooked through. Garnish with naam jim kai. **Serves 4.**

Chicken with Roasted Garlic Aïoli

Throughout Provence, garlic is so revered that annual festivals called Le Grand Aïoli honor it with platters of garlic mayonnaise, surrounded by poultry, seasonal vegetables, and sometimes fish. Tradition calls for an aïoli with the bite of raw garlic, but roasted cloves are a smooth alternative.

One 3½-pound chicken

I teaspoon salt

3 sprigs fresh rosemary

I lemon, pricked all over
with a fork

I pound small beets, trimmed &
scrubbed

3 leeks (white & tender green
parts), well rinsed

⅛ teaspoon black pepper

I pound small new potatoes,
boiled until just tender

3 large carrots, julienned,
blanched in boiling water
4 minutes & drained

2 large red bell peppers,
seeded & julienned

2 medium zucchini,
sliced ¼ inch thick

I bunch radishes

I fennel bulb, thinly sliced

Aïoli:

I garlic bulb, roasted (p. 10)

½ teaspoon salt

3 large egg yolks

2 cups extra-virgin olive oil

3 tablespoons lemon juice

Preheat the oven to 400°F. Sprinkle the chicken inside and out with ½ teaspoon of the salt. Place the rosemary and lemon inside the chicken and truss. Place the chicken, breast side down, in a lightly oiled roasting pan and roast for 20 minutes. Turn the chicken breast side up, reduce the heat to 375°F, and roast for 50 minutes longer, until the juices run clear when the chicken is pierced with a fork.

Meanwhile, wrap the beets in 2 separate packets of aluminum foil and place on a baking sheet. Bake alongside the chicken for 1 hour, until the beets are tender when pierced with a knife. Allow to cool; unwrap and peel.

Oil a large sheet of aluminum foil, place the leeks on the foil, and sprinkle with the remaining salt and the pepper. Fold the foil over and seal to make a packet. Bake for 15 minutes, turning the packet once, until the leeks are tender when pierced with a knife.

Make the aïoli: Peel the garlic. In a small bowl, combine the garlic and salt. Using the back of a spoon, mash the garlic and salt to a smooth paste. Stir in the yolks, then whisk in half the oil, drop by drop. Add the lemon juice and stir in the remaining oil until the sauce is glossy and the consistency of mayonnaise.

Arrange the chicken and all the vegetables on a platter. Serve with aïoli in small bowls alongside. **Serves 6 to 8.**

CHICKEN WITH 40 CLOVES OF GARLIC

The very idea of cooking 40 cloves of garlic would be unthinkable were it not for the fact that the garlic cooks gently ~ poaches, actually ~ turning soft in texture and sweet in flavor. Don't even think of throwing the garlic away once the chicken is cooked: Spread it on fresh bread as you would butter.

6 tablespoons butter, softened
1 tablespoon vegetable oil
One 3½-pound chicken, cut into
    8 pieces, rinsed & patted dry
Salt & black pepper

40 cloves garlic, unpeeled,
    blanched in boiling water for
    10 minutes & drained
½ teaspoon dried thyme
1 bay leaf
½ cup dry white wine
1 cup chicken broth

In a large deep skillet over medium-high heat, melt 2 tablespoons of the butter and the oil. Add the chicken, season with salt and pepper to taste, and brown it on all sides. Distribute the garlic around the chicken and season with the thyme and bay leaf. Cover the skillet and cook over medium-low heat for 30 to 35 minutes, until the juices run clear when the chicken is pierced with a fork. Transfer the chicken and garlic to a platter and keep warm. Discard the bay leaf. Skim and discard the fat from the pan, add the wine, and reduce the liquid by half over high heat. Add the broth and reduce to ¾ cup. Remove the pan from the heat and swirl in the remaining butter. Pour the sauce over the chicken and serve. **Serves 4 to 6.**

GARLIC CHICKEN

Variations on this dish are served in many New Orleans restaurants.

One 3- to 3½-pound chicken,
 cut into 8 pieces, rinsed
 & patted dry
Salt & black pepper
3 tablespoons olive oil
5 large garlic cloves, minced

1 teaspoon dried rosemary,
 crumbled
1 teaspoon dried oregano
½ cup dry white wine
½ teaspoon hot-pepper sauce
½ teaspoon Worcestershire
 sauce

Sprinkle the chicken with the salt and pepper to taste. In a large skillet, heat the oil over medium heat. Add the chicken and cook over medium-high heat, turning once or twice, for about 6 minutes, until browned on both sides. Reduce the heat to low, cover, and cook for about 25 minutes, until the chicken juices run clear when a thigh is pierced. Remove with a slotted spoon to a plate.

Add the garlic, rosemary, and oregano to the skillet and cook over medium-low heat, stirring frequently, for about 2 minutes. Add the wine and bring to a boil over high heat, stirring to scrape up any browned bits from the bottom of the pan. Gently boil the sauce for 2 to 3 minutes, until it has thickened slightly. Stir in the hot-pepper sauce and Worcestershire sauce.

Return the chicken to the skillet and cook over low heat to warm through. Serve the chicken with the sauce spooned over it. **Serves 4 to 6.**

Mole Poblano de Guajolote with cactus salad

MOLE POBLANO DE GUAJOLOTE

It is the sauce ~ the mole *~ that has made this great classic dish of Puebla,*
Mexico, world famous. Chile-based, with nuts, fruits, and chocolate,
the creation is credited to nuns, who, upon hearing that a bishop and a Spanish
viceroy were coming to the convent, prepared a dish worthy of such
important guests. Should the amount of lard concern you, substitute olive oil ~
not typical, but more healthful. This recipe yields enough sauce
to make the dish a second time; you can freeze the sauce for up to three
months. Serve this dish with a cactus, avocado, or other salad.

¼ pound lard or ½ cup olive oil

6 *chiles anchos*, stemmed

6 *chiles mulatos*, stemmed

8 *chiles pasillas*, stemmed

4 ripe plum tomatoes

½ cup thickly sliced onion

8 large garlic cloves

1 ripe plantain, peeled
& sliced ½ inch thick

½ cup raisins

¼ cup plus 2 tablespoons
toasted sesame seeds

½ cup dry-roasted peanuts

2 ounces tortilla chips
(about 1½ cups)

¼ cup white wine vinegar

9 ounces Mexican chocolate,
or 6 ounces extra-
bittersweet chocolate,
chopped

Pinch of ground cloves

½ teaspoon freshly ground
coriander seeds

1 teaspoon ground canela, or
½ teaspoon cinnamon

10 cups chicken broth,
plus additional for
thinning, heated

One 4- to 5-pound
turkey breast

The day before you plan to serve the mole: Heat the lard in a saucepan over medium-high heat. Add the chiles in batches and fry them for 1 minute, until puffed. (Do not burn or they will be bitter.) Transfer the chiles to a large bowl, setting aside the lard. Add 4 to 5 cups of boiling water to the chiles, and making sure they stay submerged, let stand for 1 hour, until softened.

In a blender, puree the chiles and 1 to 3 cups of the soaking liquid, a small amount at a time, until smooth. The sauce should have the consistency of slightly thick heavy cream. Strain to remove the solids.

Preheat the broiler. Broil the tomatoes, onion, and garlic in a baking pan 4 inches from the heat for 2 to 3 minutes, until browned. Turn the vegetables over and broil for 2 to 3 minutes, until browned. Let cool, then peel the tomatoes.

In a blender, combine in batches the vegetables, plantain, raisins, ¼ cup of the sesame seeds, peanuts, tortilla chips, vinegar, chocolate, cloves, cilantro, and canela with 2 cups of the chicken broth.

Puree until smooth.

In a large saucepan, heat the reserved lard over medium-high heat. Add the chile puree and vegetable puree and whisk to combine well, taking care that the mixture does not splatter. Add 8 cups of the chicken broth. Reduce to low heat and simmer, uncovered, stirring frequently, for 1 hour, until the sauce is thick but pourable. Remove from the heat and let stand at room temperature for 1½ hours. Cover and refrigerate overnight.

Preheat the oven to 350°F. Bake the turkey in a baking pan for 1½ to 2 hours, until tender. Let cool to room temperature, discard the skin, and remove the meat from the bones in whole pieces. Cut into ¼-inch slices, cover with plastic wrap, and refrigerate.

The day of serving the mole: In a large saucepan, heat 7 cups of sauce over medium heat. If the sauce is too thick, thin it with the additonal warm broth. Add the turkey and heat through. Serve on a platter and sprinkle with the remaining 2 tablespoons sesame seeds. **Serves 8 to 10.**

CRISPY ROAST DUCK

This recipe from southern China involves a wok, a bamboo skewer, and a two-step preparation. First the duck is air-dried ~ actually left out at room temperature for several hours as a prelude to crisping the skin. Then the bird is roasted at different temperatures for about 1 hour. The result: a beautifully burnished, almost glossy, crisp-skinned duck. Don't attempt air-drying on a hot, humid day, or even on a cold winter day when the heat is turned up. The duck should dry in a well-ventilated, cool place. Some experts recommend putting it in front of an electric fan. Not incidentally, the juice from the cooked duck, full of the aromas of ginger, scallion, and garlic, makes the perfect sauce. The bean sauce, made from fermented soybeans, and Sichuan peppercorns, is available in Asian food markets.

1 teaspoon peanut oil

4 whole scallions; plus brushes, for garnish

4 slices ginger, peeled

6 garlic cloves, crushed

2 tablespoons bean sauce

1 tablespoon dark soy sauce

1 tablespoon soy sauce

1 tablespoon rice wine

2 teaspoons sugar

1 teaspoon Sichuan peppercorns, toasted & ground

¼ cup packed fresh cilantro, plus additional for garnish

One 4- to 4 ½-pound duck, rinsed & patted dry

1 tablespoon honey

¼ cup boiling water

Heat a wok over high heat until it is hot. Add the oil, whole scallions, ginger, and garlic, and stir-fry rapidly for 1 minute, until fragrant. Add the bean sauce, both soy sauces, the wine, sugar, peppercorns, and ¼ cup of the cilantro. Bring to a boil, reduce the heat to low and simmer, covered, for 5 minutes. Uncover and let cool.

Dry the duck thoroughly with paper

towels. Remove the gizzards, neck, and liver, and any visible fat. Dissolve the honey in the boiling water and let cool.

When the scallion-soy mixture has cooled, place the duck on a roasting rack in a baking pan, breast side up, and carefully spoon the cooled mixture into the cavity of the duck through the tail end. Close the end with a bamboo skewer, "stitching" the skewer between the two open sides, and tuck in the tail end. With a pastry brush, brush the entire duck lightly with the cooled honey water. (Don't forget the underside of the duck.) Let the duck air-dry for 4 to 5 hours, until the skin feels dry and is not even slightly moist to the touch.

Preheat the oven to 450°F. Line a large roasting pan with several sheets of heavy-duty aluminum foil. Set the rack with the duck in the pan. Add cold water to the pan to a depth of ¼ inch. Roast the duck for 20 minutes. Reduce the oven temperature to 350°F and roast for 20 minutes more. Check the duck: If any part of it is browning too much, cover with a patch of foil and roast for an additional 15 to 20 minutes, until the duck is a rich brown color and is cooked through. The duck is done if the juices run clear when the meat is pierced at its thickest point with a metal skewer.

Carefully remove the duck to a platter. Remove the skewer and the solids in the cavity, and pour the juice from the cavity into a bowl. Skim the fat from the juice.

Cut the duck into serving pieces and garnish with scallion brushes and cilantro. Serve immediately, while the skin is crisp, with the warm juice as a sauce. **Serves 4 to 6.**

VINDALOO

This powerfully flavored dish from the Christian community of Goa in western India is traditionally made with pork, though lamb or beef can be substituted. For the most flavorful results, marinate the meat overnight. Tamarind paste and fenugreek seeds can be found in specialty food markets.

1½ teaspoons tamarind paste

¼ cup hot water

½ teaspoon cumin seeds

½ teaspoon black mustard seeds

½ teaspoon coriander seeds

2 bay leaves

One 3-inch cinnamon stick

½ teaspoon black peppercorns

6 garlic cloves, halved

2 medium hot green chile peppers, seeded

One 2-inch piece fresh ginger, peeled & coarsely chopped

2 tablespoons plus ½ cup olive oil

2 pounds boneless lean pork (leg or shoulder), cut into 1-inch cubes

½ cup thinly sliced onions, plus 1 cup finely chopped onions for garnish

1½ teaspoons ground turmeric

½ teaspoon cracked fenugreek seeds

2 teaspoons chile powder

1½ teaspoons ground coriander

½ teaspoon salt

½ cup apple cider vinegar or distilled white vinegar

2 tablespoons vegetable oil

¼ cup finely chopped fresh cilantro, for garnish

In a small bowl, whisk the tamarind paste and hot water together until smooth. Set aside.

Heat a heavy skillet over medium heat. Add the cumin, mustard, and coriander seeds and toast, stirring constantly, for 4 minutes, until they begin to pop. In a spice grinder or a mortar with a pestle, grind the seeds, bay leaves, cinnamon, and peppercorns until fine. Transfer to a small bowl.

In a food processor fitted with the metal blade, combine the garlic, chile peppers, and ginger until fine. Stir the garlic mixture and 2 tablespoons of the olive oil into the ground spices. Place the pork in a large bowl, add the garlic-spice mixture and the tamarind, and toss until well coated. Cover with plastic wrap and let stand for 2 hours, or refrigerate overnight.

In a large skillet, heat the remaining ½ cup of olive oil over medium-high heat. Add the sliced onion and cook, stirring frequently, for 10 minutes, until lightly browned. Add the turmeric, fenugreek, chile powder, ground coriander, and salt, and cook, stirring constantly, for 30 seconds. Reduce the heat to medium, add the pork and its marinade, and cook, turning the pork often, for 5 minutes. Reduce the heat to low and cook, stirring occasionally, for 10 minutes. Stir in the vinegar, cover, and cook, stirring occasionally, for 30 minutes. Stir in ¼ cup of water, cover, and cook for 1¼ to 1½ hours, until the pork is tender.

Meanwhile, in a small skillet, heat the vegetable oil over high heat. Add the remaining chopped onions and cook, stirring constantly, for 12 minutes, until brown and crispy.

Serve the Vindaloo garnished with the onions and fresh cilantro. **Serves 6 to 8.**

THAI PORK WITH GREEN BEANS

The influence of Chinese cooking is obvious in this
Thai stir-fry. Garlic is introduced by way of the red curry paste.
The dish is hot but not overwhelmingly so.

¾ pound boneless pork loin

1 pound green beans, cut into
2-inch pieces

2 tablespoons vegetable oil

3 tablespoons Thai Red Curry
Paste (p. 65)

3 tablespoons *nam pla*
(Thai fish sauce)

1 tablespoon sugar

Lettuce leaves

Tomato wedges & bean sprouts,
for garnish

Cut the pork into 2-inch-wide strips, then cut each strip into ¼-inch slices.

In a large saucepan of boiling water, blanch the beans for 1 minute, until bright green. Refresh under cold water and drain.

In a wok, heat the oil over medium heat until hot but not smoking. Add the curry paste and stir-fry for 3 to 4 minutes, until fragrant. Add ⅓ cup of cold water, stirring constantly, until a smooth paste forms. Add the pork and cook, stirring constantly, for 5 minutes, until the pork begins to turn white. Add the beans, nam pla, and sugar and cook, stirring constantly, until well combined and the pork is cooked through. Line a platter with lettuce leaves, arrange the pork mixture over them, and garnish with tomato wedges and bean sprouts. **Serves 4.**

THAI RED CURRY PASTE

Curry pastes are a staple of Thai cooking, used as major components in flavoring dishes. This red version, Nam Prik Gaeng Ped, *vibrant in color and hot and bold, relies on garlic and dried chiles ~ lots of them ~ for its knockout punch. Because chiles vary in size and flavor, you may have to adjust the amount to your own taste. Fresh cilantror is usually sold with its roots. You can find* galangal *(a relative of ginger), lemongrass, and shrimp paste in Asian food shops. Use this paste to make Thai Pork with Green Beans. Or, add it to soups and sauces, or as a rub for grilled chicken.*

14 small dried red chile peppers
2 medium shallots, chopped
10 garlic cloves, chopped
2 tablespoons minced fresh
   or frozen galangal
2 stalks lemongrass, thinly
   sliced
1 teaspoon white peppercorns
½ teaspoon coriander seeds
2 coriander roots
1½ teaspoons shrimp paste

Cover the chile peppers in water and soak about 1 hour, until just softened. Drain and discard the water.

In a food processor fitted with the metal blade, combine the chile peppers, shallots, garlic, galangal, lemongrass, peppercorns, coriander seeds, coriander roots, and shrimp paste until smooth, gradually adding 1 to 2 tablespoons of water to assist the blending. The paste should be smooth but not wet. Store in an airtight container in the refrigerator for 1 to 2 weeks, or freeze for up to 6 months. **Makes ½ cup.**

GRILLED LEG OF LAMB WITH GARLIC AND MINT AÏOLI

This versatile main course, made in a kettle-type charcoal grill, is ideal for backyard entertaining.

4 garlic cloves

2 teaspoons fresh rosemary

1 teaspoon black peppercorns

1 teaspoon salt

½ cup fresh mint

2 tablespoons olive oil

2 tablespoons red wine vinegar

One 3½-pound trimmed & butterflied boneless leg of lamb

Garlic & Mint Aïoli:

1 garlic bulb, roasted (p. 10)

1 large egg

1½ tablespoons fresh lemon juice

1½ cups olive oil

½ cup fresh mint, chopped

1 teaspoon fresh rosemary, chopped

½ teaspoon salt

In a mortar with a pestle, mash together the garlic, rosemary, peppercorns, salt, mint, oil, and vinegar until the mixture forms a paste. Rub the mixture all over the lamb. Place the lamb in a roasting pan, cover with plastic wrap, and let stand at room temperature for 1 hour.

Meanwhile, make the aïoli: Peel the garlic. In a food processor fitted with the metal blade, combine the egg and roasted garlic and process until pureed. In a small bowl, combine the lemon juice and oil. With the motor running, pour the oil mixture through the feed tube in a thin steady stream until combined. (The sauce will be the consistency of mayonnaise.) Transfer the sauce to a small bowl. Stir in the mint, rosemary, and salt.

Prepare a fire in a kettle-type charcoal grill. When the coals are burning white,

divide them in half and push them to either side of the grill. Place the grill rack over the coals and put the lamb, fat side down, in the center of the rack. Close the lid, leaving the vents open. Grill for about 30 minutes, until a meat thermometer inserted into the thickest part of the meat registers 135°F. (The meat will range from rare in the thicker parts to medium in the thinner parts.) Transfer the lamb to a cutting board, cover loosely with aluminum foil, and let it rest for 10 minutes.

Carve the lamb and serve with the aïoli on the side. **Serves 8.**

LAMB AND SPINACH CURRY

Spinach and lamb make good companions ~ the juices of the meat and the earthy flavor of the vegetable produce a well-balanced dish. This version, heavy on the garlic, is especially popular in Nepal and Sri Lanka.

¼ cup plus 1 tablespoon
    vegetable oil

2 pounds boneless lean lamb
    (leg or shoulder), cut into
    1-inch pieces

1 teaspoon fenugreek seeds

½ teaspoon cumin seeds

1 teaspoon black mustard seeds

One 3-inch cinnamon stick

6 cardamom pods

2 cups coarsely chopped onions

6 garlic cloves, halved

1 large hot green chile
    pepper, seeded

One 2-inch piece ginger, peeled
    & coarsely chopped

2 teaspoons ground turmeric

1 teaspoon ground cumin

1 teaspoon chile powder

1 teaspoon ground coriander

2 bay leaves

1½ pounds frozen spinach

1 teaspoon salt

¼ cup finely chopped fresh
    cilantro, for garnish

In a large saucepan, heat 2 tablespoons of the oil over high heat. Add half the lamb and cook, turning often, for 6 minutes, until lightly browned on all sides. Transfer the lamb to a plate. Add 1 tablespoon of the oil to the pan and repeat the process with the remaining lamb.

Add 2 tablespoons of the oil to the pan and heat until very hot but not smoking. Add the fenugreek, cumin, and mustard seeds, cinnamon, and cardamom, and cook, stirring constantly, for 1 minute, until the seeds pop and blacken. Reduce the heat to medium, add the onions, and cook,

stirring occasionally, for 5 minutes, until the onions are soft.

Meanwhile, in a food processor fitted with the metal blade, combine the garlic, chile pepper, and ginger, and process until fine.

Add the garlic mixture, turmeric, ground cumin, chile powder, ground coriander, and bay leaves to the onions, and cook, stirring constantly, for 1 minute. Add the lamb, reduce the heat to low and cook, covered, stirring occasionally, for 1¼ hours. Add 2 table-spoons of cold water, the spinach, and the salt. Cover and cook, stirring often, for 15 minutes, until the spinach is tender. Serve garnished with the fresh cilantro. **Serves 6 to 8.**

OSSOBUCO

*Among the widely celebrated veal dishes of Italy is this
classic recipe from Milan. Traditionally, the shanks are braised
until fork-tender, sprinkled with* gremolata *(a mixture
of lemon rind, parsley, and garlic), then served with risotto.*

4 pounds veal shanks
Flour for dredging
Salt & black pepper
3 tablespoons butter
3 tablespoons olive oil
1 large onion, minced
½ cup minced celery
½ cup minced carrot
3 large garlic cloves, minced
1 cup dry white wine
1½ cups beef broth

1½ cups canned crushed
   tomatoes in puree
¼ cup minced fresh basil
1 teaspoon dried rosemary

Gremolata:

2 tablespoons freshly grated
   lemon zest
¼ cup minced fresh
   flat-leaf parsley
3 garlic cloves, finely minced

Preheat the oven to 350°F.

Dredge the veal in the flour, shaking off the excess, then sprinkle with salt and pepper to taste. In a casserole over medium heat, brown the veal in half of the butter and oil. Remove to a platter. Discard the fat from the casserole, add the remaining butter and oil, and cook the onion, celery, carrot, and garlic, stirring occasionally, for 5 minutes. Add the wine and reduce for 1 minute. Add the beef broth, tomatoes with puree, herbs, and salt and pepper to taste. Return the veal to the casserole and bring the liquid to a simmer. Cover and braise the veal for 1½ to 2 hours, until tender.

Make the gremolata: In a small bowl, mix the lemon rind, parsley, and garlic until well combined.

Remove the veal to a serving dish. Skim the fat from the cooking liquid and reduce the sauce over high heat until slightly thickened.

Spoon the reduced sauce over the veal and sprinkle the gremolata on top. **Serves 4 to 6.**

CORSICAN BEEF STEW

From the French island of Corsica, this classic stew, also called
Pebronata, *has a rich taste and a deep burgundy color.* Pebronata
was originally a sauce added to an almost finished beef dish.
Here the sauce and meat are cooked together, producing a robust flavor.

3 tablespoons olive oil

2 pounds beef chuck, cut
   into 1½-inch chunks

Flour for dredging

2 cups chopped onions

4 garlic cloves, crushed

2 medium red bell peppers,
   seeded & diced

1½ cups dry red wine

1¼ cups finely chopped
   tomatoes

½ teaspoon dried thyme,
   crumbled

½ teaspoon salt

6 juniper berries, crushed

2 tablespoons chopped fresh
   flat-leaf parsley

Preheat the oven to 350°F. In a Dutch oven, heat 2 tablespoons of the oil over medium-high heat. Dredge the meat in the flour until well coated, then shake off any excess. Add the beef to the pot, in batches if necessary, and cook for about 5 minutes, until browned on all sides. Transfer to a large bowl.

Add the remaining oil to the Dutch oven and reduce the heat to low. Add the onions and cook for 7 minutes, until soft. Add the garlic and cook for 3 minutes. Stir in the bell peppers and cook for 5 minutes, until the peppers are almost tender. Add the wine, bring to a boil, and cook for 3 minutes. Stir in the tomatoes, thyme, salt, juniper berries, parsley, and meat, and return to a boil. Cover, place in the oven, and bake for 1¼ hours, until the meat is tender. **Serves 4.**

Pozole Rojo

*Throughout Mexico, pozole, or stew, is practically a national dish.
There are many versions, from red ones like this from the
state of Jalisco to green ones made vibrant with fresh herbs and green chile
peppers. In all of them the chief ingredient is hominy, or dried
slack corn (also called pozole). So popular are they that some restaurants
set aside their regular menus once a week in favor of pozole
night. Serve this stew as a main course with just tortillas and a beverage.*

1½ pounds dried white pozole

4 sprigs fresh oregano, or
   1 teaspoon dried

4 sprigs fresh marjoram, or
   1 teaspoon dried

4 sprigs fresh thyme, or
   1 teaspoon dried

⅓ cup lard or vegetable oil

1½ pounds boneless pork butt,
   cut into 1-inch cubes

6 to 8 *chiles de árbol*, stemmed

3½ cups coarsely chopped
   onions

8 large garlic cloves

2 large bay leaves

½ cup ground *chile ancho*

1 pound smoked pork shanks
   (optional)

16 cups beef broth

1 tablespoon coarse salt

Shredded cabbage, for garnish

Julienned strips of radishes,
   for garnish

Wedges of lime, for garnish

In a large bowl, soak the pozole in water to cover for 8 hours or overnight. Drain. If using fresh herbs, tie them together with kitchen string.

Melt the lard or heat the oil in a large stockpot over medium-high heat and cook the pork butt for 5 to 8 minutes, until browned. Add the chiles de árbol and fry, stirring, for 5 to 10 seconds. Add the onions and garlic and cook for 2 to 3 minutes, until softened. Add the herb bundle, bay leaves, chile ancho, pork

shanks if using, pozole, and beef broth. If using dried herbs, sprinkle into the pot. Bring the mixture to a boil, reduce the heat, and simmer uncovered, stirring occasionally, for about 3 hours, until the pork is tender and the pozole is puffed and chewy. Add the salt and cook for 5 minutes more. Remove and discard the herb bundle, chiles de árbol, bay leaves, and pork shanks. Serve the stew in soup bowls and garnish with cabbage, radishes, and lime. **Serves 8 to 10.**

Indian Garlic Beef with Peas

This is an easy and versatile dish ~ you can vary the spices according to taste and adjust the heat by adding more or less garlic and chile. Garam masala, a blend of several spices, and dried mango powder are available at specialty food markets. An additional tablespoon of lemon or lime juice can be substituted for the dried mango powder.

5 garlic cloves, halved

1 large hot green chile pepper, seeded

One 2-inch piece ginger, peeled

5 tablespoons vegetable oil

1 teaspoon cumin seeds

1 teaspoon black mustard seeds

1½ cups coarsely chopped onions

2 bay leaves

One 3-inch cinnamon stick

1 teaspoon ground turmeric

1 teaspoon chile powder

1 teaspoon ground cumin

1 teaspoon ground coriander

1 pound ground beef

2 medium tomatoes, coarsely chopped

1 teaspoon salt

1 cup thawed frozen peas

1 teaspoon garam masala

1 tablespoon lemon juice

Pinch of dried mango powder

2 tablespoons finely chopped fresh cilantro, for garnish

In a food processor fitted with the metal blade, combine the garlic, chile, and ginger, and process until fine. Set aside.

In a medium-size saucepan, heat the oil over high heat until very hot but not smoking. Add the cumin and mustard seeds and cook, stirring, for 30 seconds, until the seeds pop. Reduce the heat to medium, add the onions and cook, stirring occasionally, for 10 minutes,

until golden. Stir in the garlic mixture and cook for 1 minute. Add the bay leaves, cinnamon, turmeric, chile powder, ground cumin, ground coriander, and beef and cook, stirring occasionally, for 10 minutes. Add 1 cup of cold water, the tomatoes, and the salt, and cook for 5 minutes. Reduce the heat to low, add the peas and cook, stirring occasionally, for about 5 minutes, until the peas are tender. Stir in the garam masala, lemon juice, and mango powder. Serve garnished with the fresh cilantro. **Serves 4.**

HUNAN-STYLE CHILE BEEF

*Both Hunan and Sichuan provinces are known for their spicy combinations.
If you don't like your food fiery hot, decrease the peppers in this
stir-fry recipe by half, and serve with Stir-Fried Spinach with Fragrant
Garlic (p. 89) as a way of cooling things off.*

1 tablespoon rice wine

1 tablespoon cornstarch

3 tablespoons soy sauce

3 tablespoons peanut oil

¾ pound flank steak, trimmed

2 tablespoons fermented
　black beans

2 hot green chile peppers

2 hot red chile peppers

1 tablespoon finely minced
　peeled ginger

8 garlic cloves, minced

1 teaspoon red rice vinegar

1 teaspoon sesame oil

½ teaspoon sugar

Slice the steak along the grain into 2-inch-wide strips. Cut each strip across the grain into ¼-inch-thick slices. In a medium-size bowl, combine the wine, cornstarch, and 1 tablespoon of the soy sauce. Stir in 1 tablespoon of the peanut oil. Add the beef.

Rinse the beans in several changes of cold water and drain. Using the back of a cleaver, mash them coarsely. Remove the seeds from the chile peppers and slice into ¼-inch-wide strips.

Heat a wok over medium-high heat until it just begins to smoke. Add 1 tablespoon of the peanut oil and the beef, spreading it in the wok. Cook for 1 to 2 minutes, letting the meat begin to brown. Then stir-fry rapidly for 1 to 2 minutes, until browned but still slightly rare. Remove to a plate. Add the remaining peanut oil to the wok with the ginger, garlic, and beans. Stir-fry rapidly for 30 seconds, until fragrant. Add the peppers and stir-fry rapidly for 1 minute, until the

Hunan-Style Chile Beef, served with Stir-Fried Spinach with Fragrant Garlic (p. 89)

peppers are limp. Add the beef and stir-fry rapidly for 1 more minute. Add the remaining soy sauce, the vinegar, sesame oil, and sugar, and stir-fry rapidly until the beef is heated through. Serve immediately. **Serves 4 to 6.**

GARLIC MASHED POTATOES

*This is a simply heavenly version of a most traditional American
potato dish. For best results, use Yellow Finn potatoes, which are grown in
the Pacific Northwest and are available in specialty produce markets.
This recipe brings out the creamy texture and buttery flavor of the potatoes.*

2½ pounds medium Yellow
    Finn or Idaho potatoes,
    peeled & quartered

2 large garlic bulbs, cloves
    separated & peeled

¼ cup (½ stick) unsalted butter,
    softened

½ cup half & half, warmed

Salt & white pepper

Bring a large saucepan of salted water to a boil over high heat. Add the potatoes and garlic, reduce the heat to medium-high and boil gently, uncovered, for about 20 minutes, until the potatoes and garlic are tender. Drain well; set aside the cooking liquid.

Transfer the potatoes and garlic to a large bowl. Add the butter and coarsely mash the potatoes and garlic with a potato masher or fork. Make a well in the center of the potatoes and pour in the warm half and half. Using a hand-held electric mixer, beat the mixture just until light and creamy. If necessary, add some of the reserved cooking liquid to achieve a smooth, fluffy texture. Season to taste with salt and pepper. Serve immediately. **Serves 6.**

GARLIC NEW POTATO SALAD

*Red-skinned new potatoes are the best choice for this salad because
they keep their shape and texture when cooked and
quartered. With its roasted garlic flavoring, this salad makes a
delicious accompaniment to pork or duck main dishes.*

2 pounds medium
    red-skinned new potatoes
1 tablespoon salt
10 roasted garlic cloves, about
    1 bulb (p. 10)
2 tablespoons olive oil
1 tablespoon balsamic vinegar

1 teaspoon minced fresh parsley
1 teaspoon fresh marjoram
1 teaspoon fresh rosemary,
    chopped
1 teaspoon fresh thyme
½ teaspoon black pepper

Put the potatoes in a large saucepan with enough water to cover by 3 inches. Add 2 teaspoons of the salt and bring to a boil over high heat. Reduce the heat to medium and cook, uncovered, for 15 minutes, until just tender when pierced with a fork. Drain well. When cool enough to handle, cut the potatoes into quarters, transfer to a baking pan large enough to hold them in a single layer, and set aside.

Preheat the oven to 400°F.

In a food processor fitted with the metal blade, combine the roasted garlic, oil, vinegar, and the remaining salt, and process until pureed. Pour the garlic mixture over the potatoes, tossing to coat.

Bake for 15 minutes. Sprinkle with the herbs and pepper, tossing to coat. Bake for another 5 to 10 minutes, until the potatoes begin to turn golden. Serve warm. **Serves 6.**

ROYAL BEANS

Called royal beans because of their rich flavor, this nutritious dish is a great favorite with Punjabis and other peoples of northern India. Here it is prepared in a pressure cooker. Asafetida, a strong-tasting spice with a pronounced garlicky flavor, is available at specialty food markets.

2 cups dried red kidney beans, picked over & rinsed

1 cup chopped onions

5 garlic cloves, finely chopped

One 2-inch piece ginger, peeled & coarsely chopped

1 teaspoon ground turmeric

1 teaspoon ground coriander

1 teaspoon chile powder

1 teaspoon ground cumin

1 teaspoon cumin seeds

1 teaspoon mustard seeds

1 teaspoon asafetida

⅓ cup vegetable oil

One 16-ounce can whole tomatoes, chopped, with their juice

1 teaspoon salt

¼ cup finely chopped fresh cilantro, for garnish

In a medium-size bowl, soak the beans in 4 cups of water at least 8 hours or overnight. Drain; set aside the soaking water and add enough fresh water to make a total of 6 cups.

In a 4-quart pressure cooker, combine the beans, the 6 cups of water, the onions, garlic, ginger, spices, and oil. Bring to a boil, cover, and cook for 15 minutes at 15 pounds pressure, according to the manufacturer's directions. Remove from the heat and reduce the pressure quickly, according to the manufacturer's directions.

Remove the lid and stir in the tomatoes with juice and salt. Bring to a boil, cover, and cook for 20 minutes at 15 pounds pressure, until the beans are soft. Serve garnished with the fresh cilantro. **Serves 8.**

GARLIC~SAFFRON RICE

This is the special rice dish served at Indian wedding feasts and at Diwali, the Festival of Lights. The saffron and spices add a delicate aroma and the almonds provide a pleasant crunch. Traditionally, tissue-thin pieces of edible gold or silver leaf are sometimes used to decorate the rice just before serving.

1 cup basmati rice, well rinsed
Pinch of saffron threads
1½ tablespoons olive oil
6 garlic cloves, minced
4 green cardamom pods, cracked
One 3-inch cinnamon stick
½ teaspoon salt
½ cup seedless golden raisins
20 whole blanched almonds

In a medium-size bowl, cover the rice with warm water and soak for 30 minutes; drain.

In a small bowl, soak the saffron in ⅓ cup of hot water for 20 minutes.

In a medium-size saucepan, heat the oil over high heat until very hot but not smoking. Add the garlic, cardamom, and cinnamon, and cook, stirring constantly, for 30 seconds, until the seeds begin to pop. Stir in the rice, salt, raisins, almonds, 2 cups of cold water, and saffron with its soaking liquid. Heat to boiling, reduce the heat to low and simmer, covered, for 15 minutes, until the rice is light and fluffy. **Serves 4.**

Garlic-Saffron Rice served with lamb

Arroz Mexicana

*Rice was introduced to Mexico in the mid-sixteenth century by the
Spanish and has become a staple throughout the country.
Among the sopa secas, or "dry soups" of Mexico, Arroz Mexicana is
one of the most famous. Regional variations abound: In Puebla,
green peas are added. In Veracruz, look for plantains in the rice. And in
Oaxaca, black rice is made with the cooking liquid of black beans.*

¼ cup vegetable oil
1 pound long-grain white rice
1½ cups finely chopped onions
2 garlic cloves, minced

1 cup pureed plum tomatoes
3 cups chicken broth
2 teaspoons coarse salt

In a large saucepan, heat the oil over medium-high heat and sauté the rice for about 5 minutes, until opaque and just golden. Add the onions and garlic and sauté for 2 minutes. Stir in the tomatoes, chicken broth, and salt, and bring to a boil. Reduce the heat to low, cover, and simmer for about 25 minutes, until all the broth has been absorbed. Remove from the heat and let stand, covered, for about 5 minutes. Fluff the rice with a fork and serve. **Serves 6 to 8 (about 8 cups).**

ROASTED GARLIC-HERBED VEGETABLES

*Herbs, garlic, and olive oil accent the vegetables in this classic
Italian recipe. When possible, grill everything outdoors over hot coals.*

⅓ cup olive oil

1 pound red-skinned potatoes,
   cut into slices

1 red bell pepper, seeded &
   quartered lengthwise

1 green bell pepper, seeded
   & quartered lengthwise

1 large zucchini, trimmed,
   halved crosswise & each
   half quartered

2 onions, quartered

1½ teaspoons each fresh thyme,
   rosemary & oregano, or
   ½ teaspoon each dried

5 large garlic cloves, minced

Salt & black pepper

Preheat the oven to 400°F.

Pour the oil into a large shallow baking pan, add the potatoes, peppers, zucchini, onions, herbs, and garlic, and season with salt and pepper to taste. Bake the vegetables in one layer, turning them frequently, for 30 to 45 minutes, until tender. **Serves 6.**

Mushrooms Sautéed with Garlic and Parsley

In this preparation, simple, high-quality mushrooms are essential ~ supermarket button mushrooms may be too bland for some tastes. Try farmers' markets or speciality shops for more flavorful varieties.

1 pound wild or cultivated
   mushrooms, wiped clean

2 tablespoons olive oil

Salt & black pepper

2 tablespoons minced fresh
   flat-leaf parsley

4 garlic cloves, minced

Lemon juice

If the mushrooms are very small, trim the stems and leave whole; otherwise, cut them in half or quarter them. In a large skillet, heat the oil and sauté the mushrooms over high heat for 1 minute. Season with salt and pepper to taste and sprinkle with the parsley and garlic. Continue cooking briefly until the mushrooms have softened, about 2 to 3 minutes. Drizzle with lemon juice and serve immediately. **Serves 6 to 8.**

STIR-FRIED SPINACH WITH FRAGRANT GARLIC

*This quick vegetable stir-fry is particularly beautiful if you are
able to find young spinach with its pink roots and tender stems still attached;
look for it in loose bunches in Chinese produce markets. Otherwise,
use loose spinach, not the prepackaged variety, and remove the roots. Only
three other ingredients contribute to the whole here, testimony to a
very simple but aromatic combination popular throughout China.*

4 small bunches baby spinach
   with pink roots (about
   1 pound)
3 to 5 tablespoons vegetable oil

9 garlic cloves, crushed
1 teaspoon salt
1 teaspoon sugar

Wash the spinach carefully, but do not cut off pink roots or stems. Drain well.

Heat a wok over high heat until it just begins to smoke. Add 3 tablespoons of the oil and the garlic and cook for 1 minute, until golden brown. Add the spinach and stir-fry rapidly for 2 to 3 minutes, until the leaves begin to soften. Cover the wok and cook over medium-high heat for 1 minute. Uncover, add the salt, sugar, and remaining oil if the wok looks dry. Continue to stir-fry rapidly until the spinach is limp. Serve immediately. **Serves 4 to 6.**

FIERY EGGPLANT WITH THAI BASIL

Here is a robust vegetable dish that registers hot even on the Thai heat scale. It can be made more flavorful if the eggplant is first roasted over an open flame until the skin is charred, then peeled and cut into bite-size pieces. If you do roast the eggplant, add it later in the recipe, after the oyster sauce. A word about the ingredients: Oriental eggplants are the skinny long ones, lavender in color, and yellow bean sauce is a Thai ingredient crucial to this recipe; it can be found in Asian food markets.

6 Oriental eggplants
  (about 2¼ pounds)
12 small green chile peppers
5 garlic cloves, plus 1 minced
  garlic clove
10 coriander roots, chopped
½ small onion, chopped
3 tablespoons vegetable oil

30 fresh Thai basil leaves, plus
  additional for garnish
¼ cup yellow bean sauce
¼ cup oyster sauce
1 tablespoon julienned
  red chile pepper
Chile pepper flowers, for garnish

Cut the eggplants on the diagonal into ¼-inch-thick slices and set aside.

In a food processor fitted with the metal blade, process the green chile peppers, whole garlic, coriander roots, and onion until smooth.

In a wok, heat the oil over medium-high heat until hot and beginning to smoke. Add the minced garlic and stir-fry for 30 seconds, until fragrant. Add the eggplant and 10 of the basil leaves and cook, stirring constantly for 3 to 4 minutes. Add the yellow bean sauce and 2 tablespoons of cold water and cook, stirring constantly, for 1 to 2 minutes, until well combined. Add

the oyster sauce, ⅓ cup of cold water, and 10 more basil leaves. Cook, stirring constantly, for 2 to 3 minutes, until the eggplant is cooked through. Add the red chile pepper and the remaining basil leaves and cook for 1 minute. Garnish with basil leaves and chile flowers. **Serves 6.**

BRAISED CAULIFLOWER WITH INDIAN SPICES

Potatoes and cauliflower make an ideal partnership, their flavors complementing each other perfectly. In this Indian dish they are spiked with cumin seeds, garlic, chile peppers, and nutty brown onions. Garam masala, an aromatic spice mixture, is available at specialty food markets.

5 tablespoons vegetable oil

1 tablespoon cumin seeds

4 garlic cloves, minced

1 hot green chile pepper, seeded & thinly sliced

One 2-inch piece ginger, peeled & cut into very thin slivers

½ teaspoon chile powder

½ teaspoon ground coriander

½ teaspoon ground turmeric

1 medium cauliflower, trimmed & cut into florets

1 teaspoon salt

1 large potato, peeled & cut into 1-inch cubes

1 teaspoon garam masala

¼ cup finely chopped fresh cilantro, for garnish

2 tomatoes, thinly sliced, for garnish

In a large saucepan, heat the oil over high heat until very hot but not smoking. Add the cumin seeds and cook, stirring constantly, for 30 seconds, until they pop and blacken. Reduce the heat to low, add the garlic, chile pepper, and ginger and cook, stirring constantly, for 5 minutes, until fragrant. Stir in the chile powder, ground coriander, turmeric, cauliflower, and salt, and cook, covered, for 10 minutes. Gently stir in the potatoes and 1 to 2 tablespoons of cold water to prevent the mixture from sticking. Cover and cook for 20 minutes.

To serve, sprinkle with the garam masala and garnish with the cilantro and tomatoes. **Serves 4.**

WEIGHTS

OUNCES AND POUNDS   METRICS

¼ ounce~~~~~~~~~~~~~~~~7 grams
⅓ ounce ~~~~~~~~~~~~~~10 grams
½ ounce~~~~~~~~~~~~~~~14 grams
1 ounce ~~~~~~~~~~~~~~28 grams
1½ ounces ~~~~~~~~~~~~~42 grams
1¾ ounces~~~~~~~~~~~~~50 grams
2 ounces~~~~~~~~~~~~~~57 grams
3 ounces~~~~~~~~~~~~~~85 grams
3½ ounces~~~~~~~~~~~~~100 grams
4 ounces (¼ pound) ~~~~~~~114 grams
6 ounces~~~~~~~~~~~~~~170 grams
8 ounces (½ pound) ~~~~~~~227 grams
9 ounces~~~~~~~~~~~~~~250 grams
16 ounces (1 pound)~~~~~~464 grams

LIQUID MEASURES

tsp.: teaspoon
Tbs.: tablespoon

SPOONS AND CUPS   METRIC EQUIVALENTS

¼ tsp.~~~~~~~~~~~~~1.23 milliliters
½ tsp.~~~~~~~~~~~~~2.5 milliliters
¾ tsp.~~~~~~~~~~~~~3.7 milliliters
1 tsp.~~~~~~~~~~~~~5 milliliters
1 dessertspoon ~~~~~~~~10 milliliters
1 Tbs. (3 tsp.) ~~~~~~~~15 milliliters
2 Tbs. (1 ounce) ~~~~~~~30 milliliters
¼ cup ~~~~~~~~~~~~~60 milliliters
⅓ cup ~~~~~~~~~~~~~80 milliliters
½ cup ~~~~~~~~~~~~~120 milliliters
⅔ cup ~~~~~~~~~~~~~160 milliliters
¾ cup ~~~~~~~~~~~~~180 milliliters
1 cup (8 ounces) ~~~~~~~240 milliliters
2 cups (1 pint) ~~~~~~~~480 milliliters
3 cups~~~~~~~~~~~~~720 milliliters
4 cups (1 quart)~~~~~~~~1 liter
4 quarts (1 gallon) ~~~~~~3¾ liters

TEMPERATURES

°F (FAHRENHEIT)   °C (CENTIGRADE OR CELSIUS)

32 (water freezes) ~~~~~~~~~~~0
200 ~~~~~~~~~~~~~~~~~~~~95
212 (water boils)~~~~~~~~~~~~100
250 ~~~~~~~~~~~~~~~~~~~~120
275 ~~~~~~~~~~~~~~~~~~~~135
300 (slow oven)~~~~~~~~~~~~150
325 ~~~~~~~~~~~~~~~~~~~~160
350 (moderate oven)~~~~~~~~~~175
375 ~~~~~~~~~~~~~~~~~~~~190
400 (hot oven) ~~~~~~~~~~~~205
425 ~~~~~~~~~~~~~~~~~~~~220
450 (very hot oven) ~~~~~~~~~~232
475 ~~~~~~~~~~~~~~~~~~~~245
500 (extremely hot oven)~~~~~~~260

LENGTH

U.S. MEASUREMENTS   METRIC EQUIVALENTS

⅛ inch~~~~~~~~~~~~~~~3mm
¼ inch~~~~~~~~~~~~~~~6mm
⅜ inch~~~~~~~~~~~~~~~1 cm
½ inch~~~~~~~~~~~~~~~1.2 cm
¾ inch~~~~~~~~~~~~~~~2 cm
1 inch ~~~~~~~~~~~~~~2.5 cm
1¼ inches ~~~~~~~~~~~~3.1 cm
1½ inches ~~~~~~~~~~~~3.7 cm
2 inches~~~~~~~~~~~~~~5 cm
3 inches ~~~~~~~~~~~~~7.5 cm
4 inches ~~~~~~~~~~~~~10 cm
5 inches ~~~~~~~~~~~~~12.5 cm

APPROXIMATE EQUIVALENTS

1 kilo is slightly more than 2 pounds
1 liter is slightly more than 1 quart
1 meter is slightly over 3 feet
1 centimeter is approximately ⅜ inch

INDEX

Asian Roasted Garlic ~~~~~~~~~~12
Arroz Mexicana ~~~~~~~~~~~~~86
Baba Ghannouj~~~~~~~~~~~~~~~19
Bourride ~~~~~~~~~~~~~~~~~~~38
Braised Cauliflower with Indian Spices ~92
Bruschetta con Pomodori~~~~~~~~~~13
Caesar Salad with Garlic Croutons ~~~31
Chicken with Roasted Garlic Aïoli~~~~52
Chicken with 40 Cloves of Garlic ~~~~54
Clams with Garlic and White Wine ~~~22
Cold Sesame Noodles with Chicken ~~~34
Corsican Beef Stew ~~~~~~~~~~~~72
Crispy Roast Duck ~~~~~~~~~~~~59
Fettuccine al Pesto ~~~~~~~~~~~~32
Fiery Eggplant with Thai Basil ~~~~~~90
French Vegetable Soup
   with Garlic Pistou ~~~~~~~~~~~26
Garlic Chicken ~~~~~~~~~~~~~~55
Garlic Mashed Potatoes ~~~~~~~~~~80
Garlic New Potato Salad ~~~~~~~~~81
Garlic-Saffron Rice ~~~~~~~~~~~84
Garlic Shrimp ~~~~~~~~~~~~~~21
Garlic Soup ~~~~~~~~~~~~~~~25
Gazpacho a la Andaluza ~~~~~~~~~30
Grilled Achiote Shrimp ~~~~~~~~~~46
Grilled Leg of Lamb with Garlic
   and Mint Aïoli ~~~~~~~~~~~~66
Hot and Sour Shrimp with
   Cucumber Curry~~~~~~~~~~~~48
Hunan-Style Chile Beef ~~~~~~~~~~78
Indian Garlic Beef with Peas ~~~~~~~76

Lamb and Spinach Curry ~~~~~~~~~68
Marinated Garlic-Herbed Olives~~~~~15
Mexican Garlic-Black Bean Soup~~~~~28
Mole Poblano de Guajolote ~~~~~~~57
Moroccan Grilled Fish ~~~~~~~~~~37
Mushrooms Sautéed with Garlic
   and Parsley ~~~~~~~~~~~~~~88
New England Roasted Garlic ~~~~~~~12
North Beach Cioppino ~~~~~~~~~~40
Ossobuco ~~~~~~~~~~~~~~~~~70
Pozole Rojo ~~~~~~~~~~~~~~~~74
Roasted Elephant Garlic ~~~~~~~~~12
Roasted Garlic-Herbed Vegetables ~~~87
Royal Beans ~~~~~~~~~~~~~~~83
Salsa Verde ~~~~~~~~~~~~~~~~24
Scallops with Vegetables
   and Spicy Sauce ~~~~~~~~~~~44
Spaghetti with Roasted Eggplant
   and Tomatoes ~~~~~~~~~~~~33
Steamed Artichokes with
   Garlic-Basil Aïoli ~~~~~~~~~~16
Steamed Mussels Layered with
   Thai Herbs ~~~~~~~~~~~~~~42
Stir-Fried Spinach
   with Fragrant Garlic ~~~~~~~~~89
Tapenade~~~~~~~~~~~~~~~~~18
Thai Grilled Garlic Chicken ~~~~~~~51
Thai Noodle Salad ~~~~~~~~~~~~35
Thai Pork with Green Beans ~~~~~~~64
Thai Red Curry Paste ~~~~~~~~~~65
Vindaloo ~~~~~~~~~~~~~~~~~62

All photography by Steven Mark Needham
except:
back cover and p.1: Naomi Duguid/Asia Access
p.71: Alan Richardson

Recipe credits

Debra Callan:10

Brooke Dojny: 55

Georgia Downard: 13,18,32,33,54,70,87

Sandra Gluck: 19,26,37,38,52,72

Balraj Khanna: 62,68,76,83,84,92

Kathi J.Long: 24,28,46,57,74,86

Alicia Saacs: 15,21,22,25,30,88

Ann & Larry Walker: 16,31,40,66,80,81

Grace Young: 34,35,
42,44,48,51,59,64,65,78,89,90